family first+ aid

by the Nursing Staff of the

Lucile Salter Packard

Children's Hospital

at Stanford

KLUTZ®

Art Direction
MaryEllen Podgorski

Design and Production
Michael Sherman

Illustration
Elwood H. Smith

Eyes, Ears, Nose & Pen
John Cassidy

Write Us
Klutz is an independent publisher located in Palo Alto,
California, and staffed entirely by real human beings.
We would love to hear your comments regarding this
or any of our books.

KLUTZ®
455 Portage Ave
Palo Alto, CA 94306

Additional Copies
For the location of your nearest Klutz retailer, call
(650)857-0888. Should they be tragically out of stock,
additional copies of this book, as well as the entire
library of "100% Klutz Certified" books, are available
in our mail order catalogue. See back page.

Note About the Use of Trademarks
Registered trademarks are occasionally used in this
text in lieu of the chemical or generic names for vari-
ous prescription or over-the-counter drugs. This is
done in the interest of clarity. No endorsement of par-
ticular brand(s) is implied. For the record, the brand
names and their appropriate generics are as follows:
Tylenol, acetaminophen. Benadryl, diphenhydramine.
Dramamine, dimenhydrinate. Bonine, meclizine.
Band-Aids, sterile strip bandages. Popsicle, frozen ice
novelty.

IBSN 1-57054-128-0

4 1 5 8 5 7 0 8 8 8

The Very Basics

Our First-Aid Philosophy

Pay honest attention to every hurt, no matter how invisible. Never belittle someone else's pain. Never condescend. Never give aspirin to kids. Band-Aids are medical miracles. Use empathy and patience (but don't obsess). Apply flat soda pop for bad tummies and hot soup for colds and general blahs. Bananas and toast for diarrhea. Use ice for swelling and Tylenol for pain. Elevate wounds and sprains. Push fluids. Wash cuts and scrapes relentlessly. Believe in anti-bacterial ointment and NEVER underestimate the healing power of a comfortable lap, a good story, and a fine Popsicle.

P.S. We're sorry, but helmets and seat belts are absolutely non-negotiable.

When Should You Call the Doctor?

The rule here is simple: Trust yourself. You know your child. If his or her behavior is way out of line, don't spend a lot of time second-guessing yourself, just call. The nurse or doctor will ask questions about appetite, bathroom habits, and whether or not you're seeing a lot of vomiting. In addition, they'll probably want to know about two other things:

• **Activity Level.** Lethargy gets a doctor's interest faster than hyperactivity. (Lethargy = hard to rouse, not just lying down and TVish.) Another warning sign: Flip-flopping from hyper to lethargic.

• **Temperature.** In an infant, any temperature means a call to the doctor. In an older child, anything over 104° will raise flags; so will anything over 102° that won't respond to Tylenol. But understand that temperature *by itself* is a lousy indicator. Some very sick kids run nothing higher than 102° while some kids running 104° are nothing but garden-variety feverish.

When Should You Call 911?

Trust your gut. You know an emergency situation when you see it. Pick up the phone. 911 operators are almost always trained in life-saving first aid and can walk you through mouth-to-mouth or other emergency techniques if the situation in front of you is minute-by-minute serious. NEVER hang up on a 911 operator. If there are two of you at the scene, split the job up: one person on the phone, one person by the victim. Written instructions for emergency 911 types of procedures are not in this book (although you can find them in the front pages of your phone directory) because they are VERY poorly learned from written materials. You MUST take the appropriate Red Cross classes for them.

When Should You Keep Them Home from School?

We'll start with the easy stuff: Contagious things (chicken pox, real diarrhea, strep throat, pink eye, lice, scabies, etc.) are clear stay-at-homes. So are really slobbery colds, especially with a temperature. Beyond those, unfortunately, you're into the area of guidelines more than rules. Some schools, and some teachers, have policies about illness and attendance. Give the office a call. For a lot of the rest, including the always popular runny nose, you're going to have to make the call yourself. Know that no professional knows any better. Factors to consider: their misery level, the day's activities and, of course, whether or not they've done their homework.

How to Give Medicines to Kids Who REALLY Don't Want Them

According to every pediatric nurse, physician, and veteran parent who we have spoken to, the big secret to giving medicines to unwilling kids is quite simple:

There isn't one. Sorry. Everybody does it as messily and sometimes as forcibly as you do. Here are the only tips that can help:

(1) Mix Them Into Something: If *and only if* the doctor OK's it, crush up the pills or mix in the liquid with very small portions of applesauce, ice cream, jam or something similar. Never slip it to them, though. Tell them what you're doing and why.

(2) The 60-Second Rule: Don't stretch the whole experience out. Get it over with. If the medicines are prescription and important, state your case, set up a choice or two in which all the alternatives work for you, listen sympathetically to what they have to say and then, if you have to, get physical (use additional adult help if necessary). When you're done, give them a big hug, tell them how much you love them, and how much better the medicine is going to make them feel.

(3) Pills, Liquids or Chewables: If a choice exists between pills, flavors, liquids or chewables, choose the one that works best for you and your child.

Skin Stuff

Ordinary owwies, gravel burns, infections, punctures, burns, sunburn, frostbite, poison oak, ringworm, scabies, eczema, diaper rash, impetigo, fifth disease, hand foot and mouth disease, splinters, cactus, insect and animal bites, hives, blisters, warts

Head & Neck

Lice, headaches, head bonks, black eye, pink eye, something gritty in the eye, ear infections, swimmer's ear, nosebleeds, nose bonks, sinus infections, face cuts, stuff stuck in nose, stuff stuck in ears, choking, lip cuts, teething pains, pop to the mouth, fever blisters or cold sores

Tummy Stuff

Tummy aches, vomiting, motion sickness, poisoning, diarrhea, urinary tract infection, constipation

Limbs, Fingers & Toes

Dislocated limbs, breaks and sprains, smashed finger, jammed fingers or toes, ingrown toenail

General Body Blahs

Basic fever, colds, the flu and the great American runny nose, influenza, basic cough, your basic sore throat, strep throat, scarlet fever, allergies/hay fever, croup, chicken pox, seizures, night terrors and nightmares, colic, growing pains

Skin Stuff

Ordinary Owwies · Gravel Burns · Infections
Punctures · Burns · Sunburn · Frostbite · Poison Oak
Ringworm · Scabies · Eczema · Diaper Rash · Impetigo
Fifth Disease · Hand Foot and Mouth Disease · Splinters
Cactus · Insect and Animal Bites · Hives · Blisters · Warts

The Ordinary Owwie

Cleaning any cut or scrape is non-negotiable regardless of how clean the cut looks. Use a soap that has an anti-bacterial ingredient (some do, some don't; check the packaging). Unless you're dealing with a gravel burn, or animal bite, or some other extra-ordinary skin break, there's no need to scrub and scrub. One good washing should do it. No need to use alcohol or peroxide. Protect afterwards with a sterile bandage.

Gravel Burns and Road Rash

The big question here is dirt and gravel. If either are buried in the flesh the need for a full wash-out becomes critical. This can take 10 minutes and two adults. Use a soft (new) toothbrush or a washcloth and forced water out of a faucet if possible. If gravel heals into the wound, there will be a tattoo look that can last a lifetime so you can't kid around. Go straight to the doctor if there's any chance that dirt or gravel is in the face or palms, or if you just don't like the looks of the wound. As with any skin break, follow the wash-out with a dose of anti-bacterial ointment and a bandage.

How to Tell If a Wound's Infected

Red streaks coming off a wound that's a few days old are a *definite* red flag. So's a fever. If the area around the wound becomes widely reddened, quite tender, or if the wound itself becomes pus-filled — get suspicious, call the doc. One additional comment: A *narrow* belt of red around a healing wound is normal. A *wide* (and getting wider) belt is not.

Puncture Wounds

Any puncture wound from a thumbtack on up (nails, thorns, etc.) raises the tetanus shot issue. As a general rule, tetanus shots should be renewed every 10 years, but if you're looking at a dirty wound, get a new shot if the last one was 5 or more years ago. Your doc should have the records if you can't remember. Incidentally, tetanus shots protect against lockjaw — not infection. Treat puncture wounds as you would any surface wound only just a little more so: extra washing, and extra ointment, especially with thorn stabs (notoriously nasty infections).

Burns

As a rule, burns are nastier than cuts and any burn that's raising blisters, or covers a large area, or just plain looks bad, means an immediate call to the doctor. For everyday hot pan kinds of burns, run it under cold water for a solid, by-the-clock 5 minutes. If it still hurts, do 10 minutes in the cold/10 minutes in the air and repeat until it stops hurting.

Big Safety Tip: When you've got kids in the house, turn down your water heater to 120° or less .

Sunburn:
The Basic Reality

When you expose your skin to the sun, at any age and at almost any level, you're improving your chances of getting skin cancer at some point in your life. Most dermatologists wear sunblock of SPF 30 or more on exposed parts EVERY day. Copy them and do the same. Meanwhile, what to do if you've got a bad case? Try a bath of cool water mixed with a cup of Aveeno (buy it at the drugstore) or just oatmeal. Over-the-counter sprays and lotions exist (use the non-alcohol, non-perfumed kind and store them in the fridge since they feel better cool). Drink a lot of fluids. Try Tylenol or Motrin for the discomfort. Don't break the blisters or peel off the skin and buy your SPF 30 sunblock in bulk.

Frostbite

Almost always a nose, toes, fingers, or ears problem. Frostbitten parts turn white and stay white. They might be numb, tingle or just plain hurt.

What to Do? Tylenol as you begin the warm-up process (when the pain really kicks in). Bring the temperature up gradually, in warm (not hot) water. Don't rub it, or rub snow on it. Being frostbitten once does not make the limb more prone to it in the future. If it takes longer than 60 minutes to warm up and settle down, or if it blisters, call the doc.

Poison Oak, Poison Ivy

Some ugly facts you may not have known: For as long as a year, unwashed clothing that's been really exposed can give nasty cases of poison oak/ivy to people who've only touched the clothes, not the plants. (To a much smaller degree, the same story holds for roaming pets.) When the bushes are leafless, they are still dangerous (just not quite so much). People who don't react (20% of the population doesn't) can lose their immunity overnight. A typical case peaks 24–72 hours after exposure and lasts 10–14 days. Smoke from burning brush fires of poison oak or ivy can put you in the hospital if you inhale it.

What's It Look Like? Bumpy, reddish, very itchy, maybe even oozing. Often looks a little streaky.

What to Do? Stay away from it. Wear full coverage clothing if you're going to tramp around near it. If you've touched it (or just worry that you have) you've got maybe 30 minutes to really wash it out and get the exposed clothes off. Use bar soap if you can, tons of clear water if you can't. After a rash has broken out, you've got a few choices: Cool baths or compresses to the area can relieve the itching (temporarily). So can aloe gel or cortisone cream (lots of brands at the drugstore). An oral dose of Benadryl can help as well. Some drugstore sprays exist and might even help, especially if you keep them cold in the fridge. Trim fingernails on serious scratchers. Wash all exposed clothes. Call the doc for really bad cases.

Ringworm

First of all, ring-worm is not a worm, so don't panic. It's a fungal infection, related to athlete's foot.

What's It Look Like? Red, round, raised, scaly patch. Goes from nickel-sized on up. Typically found on the chest or back, but no guarantees. Sometimes the center is clear (creating the ring look). It's moderately catchy, and should raise a moderate (no more) level of concern. Usually lasts 2 – 4 weeks with treatment.

What to Do? It's treatable in many cases by over-the-counter drugs. If it fails to respond though, call the doc, especially if it's on the scalp (rare). And if you've got a cat, or a stray kitten out by the back door, check to see if it's losing its fur. If it is, you've got your culprit. Call the vet.

Scabies

An incredibly itchy parasite problem usually found on the hands, the chest, and in the moist insides of wrists, elbows and knees. (NOT on the face or scalp except for infants.) They look like tiny bug bites and usually spread from a beginning cluster or short straight line. Moderately contagious. Moderate concern level.

What to Do? Call the doc who'll prescribe something (nothing over-the-counter really works) and figure on treating the whole family (in other words, it's a hassle).

Eczema

"Eczema" is just a catchall word meaning an itchy skin reaction usually to some-

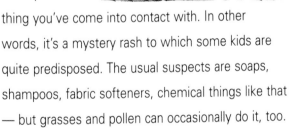

thing you've come into contact with. In other words, it's a mystery rash to which some kids are quite predisposed. The usual suspects are soaps, shampoos, fabric softeners, chemical things like that — but grasses and pollen can occasionally do it, too.

Symptoms: Mildly itchy, dry scaly patches. Typically found on the face and warm spots of your body (inside knees and elbows).

What to Do? Wash only with clear water. Use cortisone cream (drugstore), or just keep moist with plain white cream. Avoid bar soaps, perfumed anythings, and switch brands on all of your detergents, shampoos, etc. If it persists for a week or so, take it in.

Diaper Rash

An intensely red rash, often a little raw-looking, found in the (you guessed it) diaper area. Generally, baby is not happy with the situation.

What to Do? Change and cleanse frequently and gently. Vaseline is better than a wet washcloth and either is better than baby wipes. A&D or Desitin ointments can help. Give them a lot more open-air time (especially if a case of diarrhea has given you a big time problem). In general, wash baby things with mild unscented soaps and avoid plastic or rubber pants. Note: Less commonly, diaper rash is actually a yeast infection. It bothers baby less, but if you see distinct red bumps at the edge of the rash, call the doctor and be especially good about washing your hands after changing.

Impetigo

A bacteria-caused rash that looks red, raw, sometimes oozy and often with a glazed surface. Usually shows up on the face and can rip through a day-care center in no time. Usually doesn't make the kids sick.

What to Do? Only very mild cases respond to over-the-counter drugs. If you've got a case of some serious ness (in other words, it won't clear up in a week), call the doctor who'll prescribe. Check with school about attendance.

Fifth Disease

A viral rash that usually starts with a lacy kind of redness on the cheeks (gives them a "slapped cheek" appearance). Usually lasts 2–3 weeks and can be itchy. Moderately catchy. Moderate/low level of concern since kids usually don't feel very sick with it.

What to Do? Just make them comfortable. Cool compresses or anti-itch medicines exist for the symptoms, and might be helpful. Check with the school about attendance and keep them isolated from pregnant women.

Hand Foot and Mouth Disease

Another viral rash (like fifth disease) with a distinctive slightly freaky look: small blisters inside the lips, palms soles and on the fingertips (or at least near them). Moderately catchy, moderate/low level of concern since kids usually don't feel sick with it, although they can be quite miserable from the mouth sores.

What to Do? Popsicles and stories. Usually lasts 7 – 10 days. Check with school about attendance.

Splinters

Even though most wood splinters don't cause infections (exception: red-wood) you should treat them all with deep respect. They hurt big time.

What to Do? Use tweezers (or try scraping with a credit card) for any splinter that's got a bit sticking out. For those that are too small, try soaking. Make a needle your last choice and stick it in anti-bacterial ointment first. Use it gently. Don't go gouging around. If you get it out, wash the spot well and use ointment. If it's resistant to all of this, if it really hurts, or if it shows any signs of infection, call the doctor. Do NOT be embarrassed just because it's a splinter; they can be an excellent reason for a visit to the doctor.

Note: Glass splinters or fragments that are buried mean a no-questions trip to the doctor's.

Cactus or Nettle Attack

The tiny needles that cacti or nettles leave are too small to get out with tweezers. Soaking is probably the best bet, but you can also try shaving the area (razor and shaving cream).

Insect Bites:
Red Ants, Bees, Wasps, Centipedes, Horseflys, Fleas and Spiders

Although there are hundreds of bugs that sting and bite, and some hurt a heck of a lot more than others, they all get basically the same treatment. Instantly remove any left-behind stingers any way you can (seconds count). Then apply ice, raise the limb up, and wash well. If you can, apply a paste of meat tenderizer or Stingkill (it looks like chapstick and comes from the drugstore — handy stuff). Then, if you've got a bad case, cortisone cream and maybe an oral dose of antihistamine (like Benadryl) to help reduce pain and swelling. If it's on their hand and they can't wiggle their fingers, call the doc. If it's on the foot, and they can't wiggle their toes, call the doc. Any increased swelling after two days (especially beyond the nearest joint), call the doc.

Approximately 1% of the population has a potentially fatal allergy to insect stings. If your sting victim begins to wheeze after a bite, or show signs of swelling around the mouth or face, no matter where the actual sting was, get to a phone immediately and be prepared to call 911 if he or she even starts to struggle for breath.

Animal Bite

One of the more serious kinds of skin breaks.

What to Do? Clean, clean, clean for a good 10 minutes. Scrub enough to make it re-bleed. Use antibacterial ointment, then call the doctor. Animal bites that break the skin are taken seriously. Unpleasant fact: Cat bites, nasty cat scratches and human bites are all especially dirty and more prone to infection.

Avoiding Dog Bites in the First Place.

The big rule for kids is this: Don't pet or play around with strange dogs (like the kind that are on leashes tied in front of stores). Some nice-seeming dogs, especially old dogs with bad hearing, get jumpy (or just don't like kids in the first place). If a strange dog confronts you on the street, it's probably a turf thing. Don't run. Dogs will instinctively chase. Don't holler, stand very still and don't get into a stare-down. When things seem calm enough, keep an eye on him and walk slowly away from wherever the dog came from.

Ticks

Ticks are painless parasites that don't itch or draw attention to themselves (in other words, you've got to look to find them). The most recent advice regarding tick removal is quite simple: Don't use any heat on them, don't coat their tail ends with oil or vaseline, and don't try to "unscrew" them with tweezers. Just grab them with the tweezers and gently —

but firmly — pull them straight out. If they break in half — despite your best efforts at firm gentleness — try to remove the head with an alcohol-cleaned needle, same as you would for a splinter. No luck? Call the doctor.

Ticks and Lyme Disease.

Lyme disease is an infectious disease carried by ticks that can be quite serious if it is not caught in time. Only deer ticks (poppy seed – sized, about like this •) that have been in place for more than 24

DEERTICK

hours are the carriers of Lyme disease. The bigger ones, the wood ticks, are the size of watermelon seeds and don't carry Lyme. If a rash develops around a tick bite (or if it just plain looks weird after 24 hours), call the doc. Note: If you've got a suspicious tick bite, save the carcass of the removed tick in a little jar of alcohol. The doctor may want to forward it to public health for definitive diagnosis.

Hives

A lumpy red rash that can come on, vanish, and then come on again in a matter of a few hours (fastest rash in the west). The whole problem can last a week or more, but individual spots come and go quickly. Usually very itchy and the hives can show up anywhere. Typically caused by something eaten or inhaled.

What to Do? Moderate level of concern unless it's affecting breathing — which, if serious, means a call to 911. Vast majority of cases are a nuisance and no more. You can try a 24-hour course of Benadryl (an over-the-counter drug that might prevent the problem from coming on). Or just use cool compresses and sympathy.

Blisters

If the blister is small, and doesn't look like it's going to break on its own, best just to cover it with a clean bandage or moleskin (drugstore) and let it heal. If it's not small, and someplace where it's likely to break accidently, better drain it on purpose. Most kids that are old enough to get blisters are old enough to let you prick it with a sterilized needle (dip it in isopropyl alcohol). Press the contents of the blister out and wash the general area before and after really well. Leave the roof of the blister intact. It protects the raw skin beneath it.

Warts

Kids get warts. They just do. Most warts will go away in a couple of years if you ignore them (which is usually the best course). Fair warning: If a wart is a cosmetic concern, or if it just plain bothers you, the removal process is not entirely painless.

Head & Neck

Lice · Headaches · Head Bonks · Black Eye · Pink Eye
Something Gritty in the Eye · Ear Infections · Swimmer's
Ear · Nosebleeds · Nose Bonks · Sinus Infections · Face Cut
Lip Cuts · Stuff Stuck in Nose · Stuff Stuck in Ears · Choking
Teething Pains · Pop to the Mouth · Chipped Tooth
Fever Blisters or Cold Sores

Lice

Tiny parasites that
live and lay eggs in your
hair. They itch. They're
gray (kind of transparent),
they move quickly, and they're hard to find. Everybody
gets them. Nits are their eggs. They're small, white
and look a lot like tiny white teardrops. They really
stick to your hair and are a lot easier to find than their
parents. They're super-catchy and get around via
shared head things (combs, hats, pillows, towels, etc.).

What to Do? Do the class a favor and keep the lice home from school. Go straight to the drugstore and get one of the over-the-counter anti-lice shampoos. Use the comb that comes in the package and follow the directions religiously for everyone in the family. Do not ignore the part about a thorough housecleaning afterwards. If you don't do it, they'll be back in two weeks. Guaranteed.

Housecleaning tip: Things that are hard to wash (like pillows or stuffed toys) can be put in an airtight plastic bag for two weeks and that usually does it.

Headaches

Kids get headaches just like adults, although they generally won't slow down for them. If they really com-plain, try Tylenol. Or, if you want to skip the drugs, just try a quiet time-out with a cool washcloth over the eyes. Or a protein snack (cheese sticks? PB&J?). Frequent or extremely severe headaches deserve a doctor's attention.

A sudden, out-of-the-blue headache accompanied by a neck that's stiff as a board requires immediate pro-fessional attention because of the possibility of meningitis (potentially very serious). By "stiff as a board" we mean the victim has a very painful time putting chin to chest.

Head Bonks

Basic Attitude: The vast majority of head bonks are entirely innocent. But the potential for serious injury is quite present and you have to regard any bonk as significant until proven otherwise. Examine the injury with care and question the victim carefully. Lots of blood, lots of swelling and lots of tears can mean a lot — or not much at all. If the bonk was a significant one (use good sense) or if the victim behaves in any inappropriate or unusual way for the 72 hours immediately following — call the doctor. Head injuries are a good time to be over-cautious.

Infants: If the victim is an infant, raise your level of concern. Any unwitnessed fall from couch height or more that causes a blow to the head deserves a prompt call to the doctor.

Head Injury Red Flags: Here are the red flags connected to that small (but un-ignorable) percentage of head bonks that require immediate emergency attention. If you see any of these symptoms at the time of the injury, or within 24 hours of it, call 911.

- If the bleeding is spurty.
- If bleeding will not stop despite 5 solid minutes of firm pressure on the cut (no peeking).
- If the bonk puts a depression in the skull.
- If there's a blackout lasting longer than just an instant.
- If there's a seizure.
- If speech becomes confused or slurry.
- If vision gets blurred.
- If the child becomes inappropriately sleepy, hard to arouse.
- If walking is unsteady and wobbly.
- If anything liquid comes out of the ears or nose.
- If vomiting occurs more than once.

Your Basic Everyday Head Bonk

What to do? If it's not bleeding apply immediate ice (wrapped in a towel or just use a bag of frozen peas). The faster you apply the cold, the smaller the goose-egg. For the pain, Tylenol.

Bleeding? Stop the bleeding with firm, direct pressure on the cut. Use your hand, protecting the cut with a clean cloth. Tape, no matter how tight, won't do it. No peeking for 5 minutes. Caution for the squeamish: Head bonks bleed. They just do. If the cut at its widest is wider than a dime's thickness, it's a candidate for stitching. See the doctor. Once things are under control, use a good dose of the lap, story and Popsicle system.

Black Eye

Ice (or a slapped-on bag of frozen peas) for the swelling and Tylenol for the pain. You can expect a good shiner to show for at least a week and sometimes three. Fashion fact: Over a few days, the black and blue look spreads cheek-ward.

Call the doctor if: The eye is very hard to open; if it's still painful after 24 hours; if there's any bleeding into the white of the eye; or if there's any effect on the vision.

Huge Tip About Ice Bags: Buy a bag of frozen succotash for the freezer. Unlike peas, no one will ever eat it, and it will always be there for first aid needs.

Pink Eye

This is a not-too-serious but super-catchy kind of eye infection that can come on quite fast. Lots of kids wake up with it. What's it look like? One eye (or both) will be matted shut. Or maybe there will be yellow/green tearing, or redness/swelling in the lid or under the eye, or even on the white.

What to Do? Call the doc who'll prescribe eye-drops. In the meantime, clean the crusty gunk off the eyelid and lashes and wash your hands afterwards. Note: It is not uncommon to see eye and ear infections at the same time (or in combination with a cold). Total misery. Expect a long 2–3 days of it.

Something Gritty in the Eye

What to Do? Kids with something in their eye will give you, at best, only a minute or two of cooperation, so work quickly: Don't rub it. Flush the eye out with water. Get your victim to lean to one side and pour water from a glass, or squirt it from a sport bottle. Second method: Get them to open their eyes in a sinkful of warm water and look around the bottom at a few pennies you've tossed in. Third method: Pull the eyelid up and away from the eye and induce a few tears. If you can see the dirt, and it's in the corner of the eye, use a clean pinky to get it out (never use anything pointy). Call the doctor if the tears and pain don't let up after 30 minutes. (Why? The cornea may be scratched, which sounds a lot worse than it is but a doctor should look at it anyway.)

Ear Infections

The bane of young childhood. Fully half of the calls the Packard telephone nurses receive every day have to do with ear infections.

Basic Reality: Incredibly common. Problem peaks at ages 6 months to 3 years.

Symptoms: Irritability (even more than usual), crying, fussing, rubbing or poking at the ear. Hurts more if they're reclining than standing. Ear infections commonly follow a cold and will often put a kid off his or her feet. No visible skin symptoms although an infected ear will sometimes drain a cloudy fluid (don't panic) or even blood (call the doctor in either case). Sometimes a temperature, but not always.

Basic Attitude: Don't ignore (not that it's generally possible) since ear infections can lead to more serious affairs, especially for infants. Doctor has to diagnose and will usually prescribe antibiotics. Tylenol, Motrin or a warm towel from the dryer should be tried for symptoms. Sitting up is more comfortable than lying down. For quick nighttime relief of any earache that's not draining a fluid, try a few drops of room-temp cooking oil dripped into the ear. (Note: This works phenomenally well but DON'T do it if your child has had tubes implanted in his ears, anything draining from the ear, or a recently ruptured eardrum.)

Swimmer's Ear

This is an outer-ear infection that can get anybody who swims a lot (or just does a lot of bathtub scuba diving). The pain is not insignificant but there are no associated cold symptoms.

What to Do? For the pain, Tylenol. Once or twice a day you can drip a little white vinegar into the ear canal for a few minutes (assuming no implanted tubes). Reduce swimming time. If it goes three days without improvement, call the doc.

Nosebleeds

Bloody noses — either spontaneous or the result of a good pop — are quite common and only lots of uncalled-for nosebleeds over a period of two days or more generally require the attention of a doctor. Since the blood often drains back into the stomach (sorry to have to talk like this) there will occasionally be bloody vomit accompanying the problem. Don't panic. Kids who pick their noses a lot are going to have a problem here, one that's aggravated in dry weather, or in heated houses in the winter.

What to Do? Pinch the soft part of the nose (below the bridge). Hold it non-stop for 10 minutes. Tilt forward (sit down, look down at your feet). If it's an on-and-off-again, all-day kind of nosebleed, use Vaseline or neosynephrine nose drops on a wad of gauze and stuff into the nose (not too far, please, and be careful when you pull it out, so you don't disturb the scab). Need another trick? Put a dab of Vaseline in the nose at night and keep the humidifier on since dry mucous membranes are prone to bleeding. As always, if all else fails, call the doc.

Nose Bonk

If your child's had a good pop to the nose, it's BIG hurt time. If it's black and blue, put on the ice (or a bag of frozen peas). If it's black and blue and weird-looking, put on the ice and call the doctor.

Sinus Infections

A common follow-up, or miserable accompaniment, to the common cold. Gets kids and adults equally. Fair warning: It's overdiagnosed these days.

Symptoms: Pain or pressure under the bridge of the nose or behind or between the eyes. Often some swelling or dark circles under the eyes and typically thick green or yellow mucus.

What to do? Call your doctor for proper diagnosis and prescription. Plenty of fluids. Warm moist compresses. Vaporizers at night help. Try a few lightly salted water drops in each nostril if possible. A hot shower or a little towel-tent over a sinkful of hot water can relieve some of the discomfort.

Face Cuts

A caution for the squeamish: Face cuts bleed like crazy. Steel yourself. They're not life-threatening, they're just bloody. Basic rule: Any cut on the face bigger than a scratch needs to see the doctor. In the meantime, to stop the bleeding, press with something clean and don't peek for 10 minutes. Wash thoroughly with soap that has an anti-bacterial ingredient and go see the doctor for your stitches.

Lip Cuts

A cosmetic concern especially if it cuts across the "vermillion line" that defines the edge of the lips. Call the doctor. Otherwise, if it's a bitten lip or some such, apply some Popsicle therapy (the red kind hides blood well), keep an eye on it and avoid spices and citrus.

Stuff Stuck in Nose

What to Do? If it's anything organic (like paper, popcorn, a bean, a seed, etc.) move quickly, otherwise whatever it is will swell and *really* stick. If you can see it, try tweezers. (If you can't though, don't go fishing.) Whether it's organic or not, if it's out of sight, and won't come out with a few good nose blows, it's doctor visit time.

Stuff Stuck in Ears

This can be medium serious. Big Rule: If you can't see it, don't go after it with tweezers. If it's inert (pebble, bit of plastic or whatnot), try to wash it out with warm water. If it's organic — or if you don't know WHAT it is — don't use any water. Take them promptly to the doctor's (daytime) or emergency room (nighttime).

Trick Question: How do you clean the wax out of your ears? You don't. The doctor does. Do not go fishing around with Q-tips in anybody's ears. That is not what they're for. Nothing should go into the ear.

Special Note About Bugs in Ears: A bug in the ear isn't exactly life-threatening, but it can be a total freak-out of a sensation. Head straight for the doctor's or emergency room. On the way, try shining a flashlight in the ear or maybe a few drops of cooking oil (assuming no tubes implanted).

Special Note About Water in the Ears: If the usual hopping and whacking tricks don't work, put a couple of drops of rubbing alcohol into the ear (as long as the ear's owner has not had tubes implanted).

Choking for Older Kids and Adults

The vast majority of choking incidents are harmless, but nevertheless, every incident demands immediate concern and attention.

The Big Question: Can you make them talk? If they can talk — or at least make voicey kinds of noises — leave them alone. No back whaps. Adults will instinctively lean over into the appropriate position. Embarrassed, choking adults will sometimes leave a room or restaurant. Follow them. Choking victims can start out all right, and then get worse. They have to be watched. Anyone choking who has completely lost the ability to make voicey noises is an emergency situation — demanding an immediate call to the 911 operator who can walk you through the Heimlich maneuver, a life-saving first-aid procedure (also described in the front few pages of your phone directory).

Remember:

Talking = air = OK.

No talking = no air = NOT OK.

This is potentially the difference between life and death.

Choking for Babies

The most valuable step you can take in dealing with a choking baby is to prevent the problem in the first place. With that in mind, do NOT allow children under the age of 4 to eat or play with: balloons, hot dogs, popcorn, grapes, nuts, corn chips, hard candies, taffy, or thick pizza cheese. By themselves, these nine items account for a large fraction of baby choking incidents.

Having said that, babies spit up and cough all the time. The vast majority of them are normal and fine. But because of the potential for real danger you have to look at each incident carefully. Here are some guidelines: If the baby hasn't taken anything weird into its mouth, and is having just an average kind of spit-up incident, just put them on their side and let them cough it up. Pat them between the shoulder blades if need be. If there's a chance that the baby has swallowed something inappropriate, and is having what's obviously more than just an average cough and spit-up, don't panic, but get instantly vigilant and listen carefully: If the baby is making choking, voicey noises, he or she is breathing. Put them on their side and let them cough it out. If the baby CANNOT make crying voicey noises, is struggling for breath, or changing color — call 911. The operator will walk you through the emergency resuscitation process while the medics are on the way.

Teething Pains

Likelihood? 100%. It feels like a blunt blade cutting through the gums. More common at night (when there's nothing else to think about). Can affect diet.

Remedies? Prayer. Plenty of fluids. Smear a little Vaseline on the chin (prevents the dreaded "drool rash"). Rub gums with a clean finger or smear a small drop of clove oil diluted in cooking oil. Suggested chew toys: a cold teething ring, cold washcloth or frozen bagel (Zwieback makes slime). Infant dose of Tylenol for the pain.

Pop to the Mouth/Chipped Tooth

Immediate ice bag to deal with swelling. After 10 minutes or so, rinse with warm salt water and apply a Popsicle. If it's obviously serious, take them promptly into the dentist. If a tooth got chipped, bring the piece(s) with you. If you can, transport in a cup of milk.

Fever Blisters or Cold Sores

These are both basically the same thing: blisters that form on the outside of the mouth. They burn plus they're embarrassing. They'll crop up in times of stress, sunny exposure, or colds. Unfortunate fact: Once you get them, you're much more prone to getting them again. Although the herpes virus is involved, there is absolutely no moral issue connected to cold sores. **Note:** The very first time, there'll be a high fever and a _very_ sore mouth. Later attacks aren't so nasty.

What to Do? Train your child to be aware of the tingly sensation at the blister-to-be spot that comes on a day or so before the blister forms. When it does, get some ice on it right away. You can head a cold sore off at the pass. If it's too late, and the blister is already formed, put some ice on it anyway to numb it. Drugstores have chapstick-like remedies that help or you can go the prescription route (call the doc). In any event, figure on a week or so of mild discomfort and embarrassment.

Tummy Stuff

Tummy Aches · Vomiting · Motion Sickness · Poisoning
Diarrhea · Urinary Tract Infection · Constipation

Tummy Aches

Other than school-morning tummy aches, the most
common causes are weird food, gassiness, constipation, or the beginning of a stomach flu. The only
real red flag is appendicitis, which tends to come
on slowly and with pain usually pretty specific to
the right lower abdomen (these cases don't want
to walk and when they do, they're bent over). For

appendicitis is at all a suspect, call the doctor at any hour. For garden variety tummy aches, we recommend flat soda pop, daytime TV, a warm pack to the tummy, lots of rest, and a dedicated effort at pooping if that's a problem. For pent-up gas (which can really hurt) try getting them up on their elbows and knees or letting them lie down (face down on the bed) with a warm bottle on their tummies.

Vomiting

There are two kinds: Common Ordinary and Serious.

Common Ordinary Vomiting = A couple of standard episodes over the day — nothing bloody, nothing green-looking.

What to Do? Fluids. Clear soda or just water in small but frequent doses. If they can hold that down, keep it up for 4 hours. After that, increase it. After 8 hours, back to a light version of a normal diet. If they vomit again, rest the stomach and start all over again.

Serious Vomiting = Any sign of blood in the vomit (or green-looking vomit) is cause for a doctor call. Or (more commonly) 8 hours of not being able to keep a thing down (make that 4 hours if you have an infant). Because dehydration is the concern in serious vomiting, you have to raise your level of interest quite a bit if you have vomiting + diarrhea.

What to Do for Serious Vomiting? Easy. Call the doctor.

Motion Sickness

Look out the windshield (not the side windows), open the windows, don't read, keep some soda crackers in the car, chew gum, don't eat heavy meals before long drives. Many people think ginger ale (or even ginger pills) are helpful. Night driving causes fewer problems. Bonine and Dramamine are over-the-counter drugs that can help with chronic problems or really windy roads but be forewarned: both of them can make you very drowsy.

Poisoning

This is an easy one: ANY suspicious, or unidentifiable non-food liquid or solid that has been eaten or swallowed means an IMMEDIATE call to the Poison Control Center (get the number from information if you have to). That includes medicine, vitamins, coins, dirt, toys, house plants — ANYTHING funny. If the stuff came in a bottle or package, have it with you when you call so you can read off ingredients. If Poison Control wants you to make the child vomit, and you don't have ipecac in your first-aid cabinet (like you should), the Poison Control operator will walk you through a homebrew version of it. But DON'T make the victim vomit unless you're told to, and NEVER hang up on a Poison Control or 911 operator.

Ordinary Diarrhea

The vast majority of diarrhea cases are no cause for panic. A few watery stools, maybe a little vomiting or cramps. No signs of unusual lethargy or dehydration. (What are the signs of real dehydration? No peeing, a dry mouth, pasty skin.) The whole thing might last for a couple of days. Often accompanied by flu symptoms, but can come right out of the blue (maybe they ate something funny).

What to Do? You can feed them through it with small frequent doses of their normal foods, or you can try the legendary BRAT diet: <u>B</u>ananas, <u>R</u>ice, <u>A</u>pplesauce, <u>T</u>oast and the kind of yogurt that has acidophilus in it (the package will say).

Serious Diarrhea

The problem with serious diarrhea, especially in infants or very underweight children, is the potential for dehydration. You'll know serious diarrhea when you see it: It won't quit, it's very frequent, the stools are entirely watery or sometimes even bloody.

What to Do? Push non-juice, non-dairy fluids as hard as their tummies will tolerate (Gatorade works fine). If they're not vomiting, but things don't improve over 10–12 hours, call the doc. If they are vomiting, or if you just don't like what you're seeing, call sooner.

Urinary Tract Infection

Largely (but not quite 100%) a girl problem. A full-grade case means frequent peeing that REALLY hurts and burns (sometimes screamingly). The urine is occasionally bloody. A lower-grade case might just mean a very frequent urge to urinate, and "the pee won't come out."

What to Do? A prompt call to the doc (in the middle of the night if it *really* hurts). Draw a warm bath and mix in a little bit of vinegar or baking soda. Let them pee into it if they want. Don't use bubble bath; don't shampoo in the bath. Wipe from front to back with unperfumed t.p. Give your victim a lot of cranberry juice cut half-and-half with water and skip any citrus juices.

Constipation

In other words, it's painful or difficult to go. Stool is hard and infrequent. Oftentimes a problem for traveling kids, or kids just out of their home element.

What to Do? Feed them through it, with a little extra emphasis on high-fiber fruits or vegetables (popcorn for anybody over 4). Push extra fluids and the problem should take care of itself in four or five days. If it doesn't, or if you see anything really out of the ordinary, pick up the phone and call the doctor.

Limbs, Fingers & Toes

Dislocated Limbs · Breaks and Sprains · Smashed Finger
Jammed Fingers or Toes · Ingrown Toenail

Dislocated Limbs

Usually, with kids, dislocations occur in the elbows far
more than any other joint. Particularly in toddlers who
have been swung around the lawn (dads take note).

At the time of the accident, it doesn't have to hurt that much. It DOES hurt later. If your child is not using an arm after a lot of horseplay, even if the swelling is light, get suspicious. Call the doc.

Breaks and Sprains

Is it a sprain or a break? In cases in which the limb isn't obviously deformed, this can be a tricky question, requiring an X-ray for final determination. Fortunately, neither breaks nor sprains are terrifically time-sensitive and immediate care for both is quite similar.

What to Do?

Think RICE: <u>R</u>est, <u>I</u>ce, <u>C</u>ompression and <u>E</u>levation. Ice  the area immediately after the accident, rest it in a position above the level of the child's heart, and wrap it after the icing.

If the bone is actually broken the problem will aggravate over a day or two, not lessen. Severe difficulty in moving any joint is also very suspicious. If it's point sensitive ("It hurts right HERE!") call the doc. Note about toddlers and bones: Any toddler limping after a fall deserves a very close look since kids that age don't sprain very easily. (And to prevent broken legs in toddlers in the first place, don't have any car wrecks and don't let them stand up in grocery carts.)

Smashed Finger

For a seriously smashed finger (car door quality) try hard to get it into cold water and keep it there to hold down the swelling. (This is highly recommended, but it's not life or death if your patient REALLY doesn't like it.) Breaks, fortunately, are not that common. If the blood is under the nail, and not bleeding out, you have a special problem. Pressure will build up and the pain will double in short order. Head for the doctor. For less serious cases, after the cold soak (10 minutes or so), ointment and wrap everything with a big clean bandage. Then keep a good eye on it. If the pain isn't gone or it's obviously not healing in 24 hours, call the doctor.

Jammed Fingers or Toes

If the finger is movable, it probably means it's not broken, but it's no guarantee. A broken finger or toe that's not looked at for a day or even two is not that big a deal. Broken fingers are sometimes not even cast, but a jammed finger that is numb, tingles, or has gone to sleep means a call to the doc.

What to Do? Immediate ice. Tylenol for the pain. After a day, if the swelling won't come down, or the pain won't go away, call the doc. In the meantime, try buddy-taping (tape the hurt finger to a good finger). And use hard-toed shoes if you're nursing a jammed toe.

Ingrown Toenail

Don't laugh, this can be serious, making walking very painful. If the toenail dives under the skin, and hurts like crazy, don't try to cut it out. If it's oozing anything, use anti-bacterial ointment on it. Soak it three times a day in Epsom salts and warm water. If you're lucky, a day or two of soakings will let it get better on its own. No luck? Call the doc and don't be embarrassed. Any red streaking up the foot, or real swelling, really call the doc. The best cure is prevention: ALWAYS cut your nails straight across and skip the pointy-toe high heel look.

General Body Blahs

Basic Fever · Colds · The Flu & the Great American Runny
Nose · Influenza · Basic Cough · Your Basic Sore Throat
Strep Throat · Scarlet Fever · Allergies/Hay Fever
Croup · Chicken Pox · Seizures · Night Terrors
and Nightmares · Colic · Growing Pains

A General Word About Drugs

Anybody, kids or adults, can react to drugs in unexpected ways. If you see a strange reaction to any drug — either over-the-counter or prescription — immediately stop using it and call the doctor.

Basic Fever Information

We'll start this section by re-emphasizing that the exact number on a thermometer is a very unreliable measure of how sick a child really is. Some very sick kids come in with a temp of 101°, other kids can have 103° and be suffering nothing more than a garden-variety fever. In practice, nurses don't get nervous (about older kids) until they hear 104°. What DOES impress them is serious lethargy. A really zoned-out child running ANY kind of temp means a quick call to the doctor. (And by zoned-out, we don't mean just low energy and snacks in front of the TV, we mean really flattened out.)

What to Do? Put your hand on the forehead of any child older than an infant who seems feverish. You'll know if he or she is hot (for infants, use a rectal thermometer). For the ordinary low-grade fever, with no other weird signs, go into your sympathy and comfort mode — plus a little Tylenol or Motrin (NOT aspirin). The problem should take care of itself, or change into something you can recognize within a day or so. If it doesn't, or if it gets worse, pick up the phone.

If you're looking at something beyond an ordinary low-grade fever, if they're looking gray, or really burning up, or just acting strange — raise your concern level. Try an appropriate dose of Tylenol or Motrin (not for infants under 6 months, unless O.K. by doctor), and maybe a room temperature bath, but if you don't see some fairly quick improvement call the doc.

Fevers in Infants: Always use a rectal thermometer with infants. If they're under 3 months, and running any temperature, call the doctor. If they're over 3 months, and they're running a small temp (38^0C or 100.4^0F) *but otherwise nothing seems out of the ordinary*, go into your comfort measures (try Tylenol). If the temp won't come down, or if you just don't like what you're seeing, call the doc.

Note: Never try to reduce a fever with an alcohol bath.

Colds, the Flu and the Great American Runny Nose

Colds (and their runny noses) are viral — in other words, the root cause is beyond the reach of modern medicine. A hopeful point: If the nose is running, your victim is improving. It's the stuffed-up noses that can be more of a problem.

Cold symptoms that get progressively worse for 72 hours or more, or are accompanied by a cough that won't go away, present the chance of things a bit more serious. Call the doc.

If your cold sufferer's neck is board stiff, in other words head and neck have to be moved as a unit, call the doc immediately because of the chance of meningitis. Rare but serious.

Influenza (the Flu)

How do you tell the flu from a cold? It actually doesn't make a whole lot of difference since the treatment is basically the same, but a flu typically gives you full-body blahs along with standard cold symptoms.

Cure to the Flu and Common Cold? Prevention. Colds are best passed by contact, not airborne. Keep that in mind when a cold sufferer hands you the phone. People who wash their hands religiously get fewer colds (true story). Use a dishwasher. Winter is cold season not because a draft gives you a cold, but because more people (and more germs) are packed more closely together. Don't cover a sneeze with your hand. Move off by yourself and sneeze into the corner of a room.

HI!

What to Do? For kids over 6, you can try over-the-counter decongestants or Tylenol for the symptoms, bu[t] expect no miracles. Lots of chicken soup, lots of rest and lots of fluids. Steamy hot showers or baths are goo[d] temporary relief. Humidifiers in the bedroom are proba-bly more mess than they're worth. Your call. Activity level is self-determined. School? The first day or two ar[e] the catchiest. Use good judgment. Vaseline under the nose keeps it from chapping. Tissues are better than hankies because you can throw them away. Explain (probably futilely) how hopeless it is to fight a stuffy nose. Preach the "breathe through your mouth" story a[s] the alternative and remember this ugly, ugly fact: Six to ten colds a year is about typical for a child.

For Infants: Try a few drops of lightly salted warm water in each nostril, using an eyedropper. Wait a minu[te] and then use it to suck out. At night, prop them up a lit-tle more if their cribs adjust that way (don't use pillows[)]

Basic Cough

Coughs are nature's way of clearing out the lungs and aren't by themselves a bad thing (it's just that they're frequently a part of a viral infection or at least something bigger).

What to Do? Sympathy. Warm mist, warm fluids, bath[s.] If it's a dry hacking cough that's keeping them awake (o[r] making them throw up), check with your doctor. If your child is older than 12 months you might be able to try a[ ] cough medicine that has DM in it (there are lots that ar[e] over-the-counter).

At night, prop them up with a humidifier going in the room. Note: Butterscotch candies taste better than cough drops and we think they work better too.

RED FLAG

Call the doc if the cough goes on for more than a week.

Your Basic Sore Throat

Most sore throats are viral, beyond the reach of modern medicine but not beyond the reach of sympathy, warm tea, chicken soup, or Popsicles. If you've got one of those rare kids who will gargle, frequent warm salt water gargling is a great help (1/4 teaspoon per glass warm water). Over-the-counter throat sprays are mostly psychological. An appropriate dose of Motrin or Tylenol might help. If they REALLY can't swallow, they'll drool and you should call the doctor. Otherwise, your level of concern for cold-associated sore throats is pretty low. Exception: If they're getting sicker and sicker, running a fever, call the doc.

First-Thing-in-the-Morning Sore Throats

Mornings, especially school mornings, are popular times for minor sore throats. These are generally a consequence of mucus draining on the back of the throat from a case of the sniffles. When you get vertical, it's much less of a problem. Hot chocolate often takes care of it.

Strep Throat

Here's the story on strep (which, unlike your Basic Sore Throat, actually *can* be helped by antibiotics). Any nasty sore throat without cold symptoms that does not go away in a couple of days is slightly more suspicious for being strep.

Additional Symptoms: Headache, stomach ache, nausea, vomiting, a white patch on the tonsils, a fine rash on chest resembling sandpaper ... just one of thes can be the only symptom. Note though that the only dead-sure way to diagnose it is with a lab test. Strep is very catchy (not airborne but by contact) and can come on within 24 hours.

What to Do? Call the doctor who'll test for it and, if positive, will prescribe. Meanwhile, for the pain, try Tylenol or Motrin, Popsicles and stories. School? They'l be catchy until they've been on antibiotics for 24 hours

Scarlet Fever

Scarlet fever is a strain of strep throat that also shows a sandpaper chest rash (which makes it a lot easier to diagnose). It usually doesn't itch and will run you a fever along with a nasty sore throat and the rest of the strep symptoms.

What to Do? Typically, the victim is already on anti-biotics for the strep, but call the doctor anyway.

Allergies/Hay Fever

You probably know if your child is allergic to some-thing, although (unpleasant fact) allergies can develop quite suddenly at any age. You can typically distinguish an allergic reaction from a cold by the fact that the eyes itch and give a watery discharge more with an allergy, and the drainage from the nose is profuse and clear. Plus, in kids at least, you'll often see dark circles under the eyes.

If you're lucky, you'll be able to remove the source of the allergy (cats? wool? or some kind of food?) from the environment. Frequently, though, the problem is more general (pollen, seeds, dust, etc.). It might be worst in the spring, but it could very well be an all-year on-and-off-again problem. Groan. See your doc (and then, maybe, an allergist) if it really begins to interfere with your day-to-day.

Croup

Almost always a viral infection of the respiratory system that typically hits kids between the ages of 6 months and 3 years (after that, they start getting laryngitis). Mostly a spring/winter and mostly a nighttime problem. It has a distinctive (scary) sound. Very noisy on the intake and on the out-take it sounds like a barking seal. Your level of concern should be medium high.

What to Do? During the day, give the doctor a call and go over the symptoms. At night, throw them in a hot shower or have them sit in a steamy bathroom. If that doesn't work, try cold night air for 10 minutes. If neither of those help, or if the breathing becomes even close to a struggle, go to the Emergency Room or call the doctor regardless of the time. If you're looking at nothing but a mild case, try Tylenol for the fever. Warm liquids. Lots of sympathy. It's medium contagious. You don't need to isolate the sibs, but take contact precautions (in other words, don't let them share cups and such). The whole thing lasts a few days.

Chicken Pox

Getting chicken pox is almost a requirement for being a kid (which is, incidentally, the best time of life to get it). It's not hard to diagnose (ask any veteran parent). Most obvious symptom: small red bumps that change to water blisters and develop in bunches all over the body. The bumps form, break, crust over, and a new crop starts over. Very itchy and very, very contagious until they're all crusted over (takes about 7–10 days).

Level of Concern? Moderate. Occasionally a child will run a high fever for the first few days. Onset is a few symptomless pimples. Or, a few cold-like symptoms might precede. If your child is exposed, stand by, it's a 14 – 21-day incubation period. Some kids get full-blown, absolutely miserable cases ... others just get a small crop of pimples with few or no other symptoms.

What to Do? Call the doctor if the fever doesn't respond to Tylenol, or if there's a headache, vomiting, or inappropriate behavior. Otherwise, lukewarm baths every few hours (toss in a little baking soda if you can). Or you can try Benadryl, an over-the-counter drug taken orally, for the itching. Or try an anti-itch lotion from the drugstore. Keep the sufferer at home for six days after first rash, or until the pimples dry out. Some kids get the pimples in their mouths. If so, swish with Maalox (over-the-counter) and spit. No diet restrictions unless the mouth is infected, in which case avoid salty or citrus. Infants or young kids who have chicken pox need to have their fingernails cut short so they can't scratch to bleeding or scratch off the scabs and create scars. It's the rare child who hasn't had a case by 10. A vaccine is now available. Check with the doc.

Seizures

Seizures can be very serious or no big deal. (The major are fever-based and frighten the onlooker more than threaten the victim, who will be rolling their eyes back twitching or jerking their entire body.)

What to Do? This is easy. Call 911 unless you know exactly what's going on and know why you don't need emergency help (in other words, the seizure victim is y child and you're entirely familiar with his or her situation and history). If you're confronted with a seizure, while you're waiting for the paramedics, arrange the victim or his or her side if possible. Children in seizures don't sw low their tongues, but tongues can fall back and block their airways, so a lying-down-on-the-side posture is be If they come out of it before the medics arrive, reassur them (they'll probably be very sleepy). Don't give them anything to eat or drink.

Night Terrors and Nightmares

Night terrors usually happen in the first couple of hours of sleep and are significantly more frightening than nightmares, if only to the parents. Victims will scream and thrash terrifyingly. Unlike nightmares, night terrors happen in the deepest part of sleep and victims should not (actually, can not) be woken from them. All you can do is cuddle, reassure and take comfort from the fact that night terrors are very rarely remembered. Fact: Neither night terrors, nor nightmares, represent deep-seated neuroses of any kind, nor are they connected to diet.

Colic

Frequent, no-apparent-reason crying in kids between the ages of 2 weeks and 3 months is often colic. Your pediatrician should be consulted if you think you're the lucky owner of a case of colic, since a small percentage of the cases have to do with a lactose intolerance — in which case changing a breast-feeding mom's diet can actually help. Much more commonly though, the root problem seems to be connected with immature digestive or nervous systems. In other words, this is not a first- aid situation. More a state of life.

What to Do? Prayer. Long walks. Cuddle as much as you can. Setting a bassinet on a dryer is easier than

going on a car ride, or try a warm bottle of water to the tummy. If you're breast feeding, avoid spices and caffe (although the connection between mom's diet and baby colic is far from proven). Bottle feeding? Make a little p permint water by melting a peppermint candy into a bo

Remember: Crying associated with colic does not refle on the parents nor does it leave permanent scars. Be s to prescribe therapies for the caretaker, especially if it's Take long showers with the door closed. (They're terrifi You can't hear a thing.) Or hire a veteran baby-sitter and a candlelit restaurant dinner for two.

Growing Pains

For lots of kids, this is a real nighttime problem, not ps logical, and should be taken seriously. Happens anytime from 5 or 6 to puberty and is connected with bone grow and muscle spasms.

What to Do? Tylenol (or ibuprofen), warm baths, hot w bottle and sympathy. Note: A safe hot water bottle can fashioned with a wet washcloth put in a plastic baggie microwaved.

Who wrote this book...

The Parent Information and Referral Center Nurses at the Lucile Salter Packard Children's Hospital at Stanford.

James Cisco, M.D.

Lorry Frankel, M.D.

Robert Daugherty, M.D.

Gail Burton, R.N.

Bernd Kutzscher, M.D.

Marilyn Kutzscher, M.D.

Heidi Fleischmann, M.D.

Jim Scott, M.D.

Suzanne Gooding, R.N.

Deb Robinson, R.N.

Susan Robinson, R.N.

Elizbeth Sterling, R.N.

Lorna Aliperti, R.N.

Debbie Fields, R.N.

Pam Lundy, F.N.P.

Colleen Patell

Sally Schuman